FOOTBALL FOCUS

THE BUSINESS OF FOOTBALL

Clive Gifford

WAYLAND

First published in 2009 by Wayland

This paperback edition updated and published in 2011 by Wayland

Copyright © Wayland 2009

Wayland
338 Euston Road
London NW1 3BH

Wayland Australia
Level 17/207 Kent Street
Sydney, NSW 2000

Editor: Julia Adams
Produced by Tall Tree Ltd
Editor, Tall Tree: Jon Richards
Designer: Ben Ruocco

British Library Cataloguing in Publication Data

Gifford, Clive.
   The business of football. -- (Football focus)
   1. Soccer--Management--Juvenile literature.
   I. Title II. Series
   796.3'34069-dc22
ISBN: 9780750266932

Printed in China

Wayland is a division of Hachette Children's Books, an Hachette UK company. www.hachette.co.uk

Acknowledgements
The author and publisher would like to thank the following people for their help and participation in this book: Whiteknights FC, Eric Burrow, Steve Rendell and Paul Scholey

The website addresses (URLs) included in this book were valid at the time of going to press. However, because of the nature of the Internet, it is possible that some addresses may have changed, or sites may have changed or closed down since publication. While the author and Publisher regret any inconvenience this may cause the readers, no responsibility for any such changes can be accepted by either the author or the Publisher.

Picture credits
t – top, l – left, r – right, b – bottom, c – centre
cover t – Dreamstime.com/Berlinfoto, tr – Dreamstime.com/Photoplanet, br – Dreamstime.com/Benjamincoppens, bl – Dreamstime.com/Chunni4691, tl – Dreamstime.com/Diademimages, c – Dreamstime.com/Josefbosak, 1 Dreamstime.com/Albo, 2 Dreamstime.com/Diademimages, 4 Dreamstime.com/Matt Trommer, 5 Dreamstime.com/Camhi Franck, 6 Dreamstime.com/Andrea Presazzi, 7 Dreamstime.com/Diademimages, 8 Dreamstime.com/Diademimages, 9 Dreamstime.com/Robert Howarth, 10 Eddie Keogh/Reuters/Corbis, 11 Matthew Ashton/AMA/Corbis, 12 Dreamstime.com/Kojoku, 13 Dreamstime.com/Mitchell Gunn, 14 Dreamstime.com/Albo, 15 Ben Radford/Corbis, 16 Dreamstime.com/Diademimages, 17 Ben Radford/Corbis, 18 Dreamstime.com/Mitchell Gunn, 19 istockphoto.cpm/Dan Barnes, 20 Matthias Schrader/epa/Corbis, 21 Catherine Ivill/AMA/Corbis, 22 Stephane Reix/For Picture/Corbis, 23 Stephane Reix/TempSport/Corbis, 24 Matthew Ashton/AMA/Corbis, 25 Peter Morgan/Reuters/Corbis, 26 Ahmad Yusni/epa/Corbis, 27 Dreamstime.com/Ken Durden, 28 Ciro Fusco/epa/Corbis, 29 Dreamstime.com/Melissad10, 30 Matt Brown/isiphotos.com/Corbis, 32 Dreamstime.com/Diademimages

CONTENTS

The world's game

Football is the world's most popular team sport. It is played and watched by hundreds of millions of people who are attracted to its constant action, moments of drama and the skills of its players.

Business beginnings

When football developed in Britain in the mid-1800s, it was an amateur sport played mainly for fun. As the game increased in popularity, players were initially paid expenses for travel and then for time away from work. Gradually, footballers became professional, paid to play the sport full-time. At first, their wages were funded by fans paying to watch their heroes play. As football has boomed, millions of fans are drawn to watch matches live at football grounds or on television, and this generates large sums of money. This money has seen certain clubs grow into giants, while top footballers have become global stars and multi-millionaires.

ON THE BALL

In 1871, teams paid £1 to play in the first major cup competition, the English FA Cup, and there was no prize money. In the 2009-10 season, the winners received £2.7 million.

Players from Real Madrid celebrate winning the 2007–08 Spanish league title. Winning league and cup competitions provides clubs with large sums of money.

Brazilian football fans watch a game between Botafogo and Flamengo at the Maracanã stadium in Rio de Janeiro, Brazil, in 2008. Football in South America is controlled by the *Confederación Sudamericana de Fútbol* (South American Football Confederation), or CONMEBOL.

Organising football

In 1904, the *Fédération International de Football Association* (FIFA) was formed with just seven member countries (France, Belgium, Denmark, the Netherlands, Spain, Sweden and Switzerland). Today, FIFA has more than 200 member countries and runs football around the world. This includes the planet's biggest tournament, the World Cup. Each continent also has its own organisation that runs competitions. In Europe, the Union of European Football Associations (UEFA) runs competitions such as the European Championships and the Champions League. In Asia, the Asian Football Confederation (AFC) runs the Asian Champions League. Africa's organising body is the Confederation of African Football (CAF), and it runs the African Champions League for clubs and the African Cup of Nations for national teams.

> *I take pride in the fact that people go home having felt that for 90 minutes today, life is beautiful and that's it, basically. That's why professional football exists.*
>
> Manager of Arsenal,
> **Arsene Wenger**

The football industry

Football today is a sport dominated by money. The biggest clubs need money to buy the best players so that they can become more successful. They raise money from fans and from commercial agreements.

The big leagues

All of the 20 richest clubs, except Fenerbahçe in Turkey, are found in the world's five biggest leagues. These are the German *Bundesliga*, the French *Le Championnat*, the English *Premier League*, *Serie A* in Italy and *La Liga* in Spain. There is far less money in women's football, with most female players earning only part of their income from playing football. There are professional female leagues in Germany, Sweden and, from 2009, Women's Professional Soccer (WPS) in the United States.

Players of AC Milan (in red), one of the richest clubs in the world, take on Udinese in the Italian Serie A league in 2008.

The rest of the world

Elsewhere, football leagues are booming in popularity, especially in the United States, China, Japan and South Korea. African and South American leagues continue to produce top-class footballers, but clubs struggle to keep hold of them.

Many of the world's best players are not European, but come from South America, Asia and Africa. These footballers are drawn to play for clubs in Europe, attracted by high wages and the chance to play against other top players.

Money box
Richest clubs by income, 2009–10

1. Real Madrid (Spain) .... £359.1 million
2. Barcelona (Spain) .... £325.9 million
3. Manchester United (England) .... £286.4 million
4. Bayern Munich (Germany) .... £264.5 million
5. Arsenal (England) .... £224.4 million
6. Chelsea (England) .... £209.5 million
7. AC Milan (Italy) .... £193.1 million
8. Liverpool (England) .... £184.5 million
9. Inter Milan (Italy) .... £184.1 million
10. Juventus (Italy) .... £167.8 million

Source: *Deloitte Football Money League*, 2011

Two players contest a ball during a 2008 Major League Soccer (MLS) match between DC United (in black) and Toronto FC. Since it started in 1996, MLS has spread its business base from ten teams in just one country to 15 teams in both the United States and Canada.

Football fans

Football teams rely on fans to support them during matches and to raise money. Fans contribute to a club by paying for tickets to watch games and by buying club merchandise, such as replica shirts.

Club football

During a season (all the games played in one year), fans will travel all over a country to follow their club in action away from their home stadium. Many fans will also buy a season ticket costing hundreds of pounds. This allows them to go to all the matches in their team's own stadium. These matches are known as home games. With match ticket prices costing up to £60, football clubs can raise a lot of money from selling tickets, especially if they can attract crowds of more than 50,000 fans to each game.

Italian fans celebrate winning a match during the Euro 2008 finals. The money raised from ticket and merchandise sales from international matches goes to international bodies, such as UEFA, and national organisations.

Supporters' clubs

Most clubs have supporters' clubs that organise tickets and travel to games. Bayern Munich, for example, has more than 2,500 club branches with more than 190,000 paying members, making it the most organised supported club in Germany. All of the money raised from fans can make up a large part of a club's income. In the case of small clubs, money from fans may be the only source of income. Larger clubs are able to raise money from other sources, such as television and sponsorship.

ON THE BALL

For the 1998-99 season, Beryl Owen made the 700-km trip from her home to the St James Park stadium, Newcastle, for every match, even though she could not get a ticket.

An upset fan sits alone after his team has lost. Even if a team is performing poorly, fans will still pay a lot of money to support it. During the 2008–09 season, for example, the average cost of an English Premier League season ticket was £590.

Money box
Highest average attendances per game in Europe (2009-10 season)

	CLUB	GROUND	AVERAGE ATTENDANCE
1.	F.C. Barcelona (Spain)	Camp Nou	78,000
2.	Borussia Dortmund (Germany)	Signal Iduna Park	77,248
3.	Real Madrid (Spain)	Santiago Bernabéu	75,133
4.	Manchester United (England)	Old Trafford	74,864
5.	Bayern Munich (Germany)	Allianz Arena	69,000
6.	Schalke 04 (Germany)	Arena Auf Schalke	61,327
7.	Arsenal (England)	Emirates Stadium	59,927
8.	Hamburg (Germany)	AOL Arena	55,240
9.	Inter Milan (Italy)	San Siro	55,149
10.	Benfica (Portugal)	Estádio da Luz	50,033

Source: *IPAM*

Club owners

Football club owners are responsible for the business side of a club. Their roles will vary from club to club, but they may be involved in negotiating contracts with sponsors or agreeing fees to buy players.

Forms of ownership

Football clubs are owned in lots of ways. Some sell shares on stock exchanges and are owned by the shareholders who appoint a board to run the club. Others are owned by thousands of members.

Clubs such as Barcelona and Real Madrid in Spain and Yokohama FC in Japan have elections every few years where their members vote on who should run the club. In Mexico, media company Televisa owns not only the national stadium, the Azteca, but also three major football clubs: San Luis FC, Club América and Club Necaxa. In 2008, an offer to buy Club Necaxa for around £15 million came from the Mexican state government of Aguascalientes.

Some clubs are owned by very wealthy individuals. Russian oil tycoon Roman Abramovich bought English Premier League club Chelsea in 2003 for £140 million and has since spent more than £450 million on players.

ON THE BALL

Philip Anschutz of the United States owns stakes in three clubs: the LA Galaxy and Houston Dynamo in the MLS, as well as Hammarby in Sweden.

Taking over a club

Football clubs regularly change owners. In recent years, English Premier League clubs Liverpool, Manchester United and Aston Villa have all been taken over by American businessmen. Manchester City was first bought by the former Prime Minister of Thailand, Thaksin Shinawatra, and then, in 2008, by the ruling family of Abu Dhabi. Clubs from lower leagues have also attracted new owners who are keen to buy a team for a lot less money than a top-flight club. In 2007, English Championship club Queens Park Rangers (QPR) changed owners. It is now owned by Lakshmi Mittal, the fifth richest man in the world, and Formula One bosses Bernie Ecclestone and Flavio Briatore.

" I see it as part of my role as chairman to make sure we have the maximum funds as we can to be as competitive as possible. It is my duty to be on the lookout for investors. "

Director of
Tranmere Rovers,
Lorraine Rogers

QPR owners Lakshmi Mittal (second from left) and Flavio Briatore (third from left) stand alongside former QPR players (from left to right) Gerry Francis, Les Ferdinand and Paul Parker at a ceremony to unveil the club's new badge in 2008.

Managers and coaches

The person in charge of a team is called a manager or coach. Both coaches and managers are involved in training players for matches. Managers, however, are also involved in some of the business aspects of a club, such as buying and selling players.

The merry-go-round

Managers and coaches are vital to the success of a team. They decide who plays and what tactics to use. These are key to how successful a team will become – the more games a club wins, the more prize money it collects and the more fans come to see it play, earning the club even more money. The pressures to succeed at the biggest clubs are immense and, if a coach is unsuccessful, they may be dismissed by their club.

Since 1990, Real Madrid has had 20 different managers, including Gus Hiddink (left), who went on to manage Australia, South Korea and Russia.

Head of a team

A manager or coach will be the head of a large backroom team at a club. This team will include skills and fitness coaches who train the squad as well as reserve and youth teams. Physiotherapists treat injured players, while nutritionists advise on players' diets. Some managers also employ other experts. Luiz Felipe Scolari, former manager of Brazil, Portugal and English club Chelsea, has employed the same sports psychologist, Regina Brandao, for his teams for the past 12 years.

> *The most important person in any club is the manager. They make or break it. If they buy the wrong players, or get them playing the wrong way, they bankrupt you.*
>
> Managing Director of Birmingham City, **Karren Brady**

The coaching team of Manchester United during the 2008 Champions League final. For the 2008–09 season, manager Sir Alex Ferguson (third from right) led a team of 16 coaching staff, including goalkeeping coaches, scouts and team doctors.

The stadium and staff

Owning a large football stadium means that a club can attract thousands of paying fans to watch matches. However, a stadium is expensive to build and maintain and needs hundreds of workers to run it.

Moving grounds

As football has boomed in popularity, many clubs move away from their old stadiums to bigger, more modern grounds. English Premier League side Arsenal moved a short distance in London from their 38,419-seat Highbury ground to the new 60,432-seat Emirates stadium. Other sides have moved farther afield in search of new fans. For example, English side Wimbledon moved 110 kilometres from London to Milton Keynes in 2003 to attract more fans to watch games.

Some teams share a large stadium in order to save on costs. Italian Serie A clubs AC Milan and Internazionale share the 85,000-seater San Siro stadium.

> *The football ground is my arena, my colosseum, and it doesn't matter if I am fighting lions or men, I feel like I am the gladiator.*
>
> Siena striker, **Massimo Maccarone**

Club workers

A stadium needs many people to run it on match day, from stewards who deal with seating to staff selling tickets at the box office. Away from the game, a club is a major business, employing staff to market and promote the club, run its website, handle its finances and organise the sales of shirts and other souvenirs. Ground staff look after both the stadium's pitch and the pitches at the training ground, while visitor tours of a club's stadium are often led by famous ex-players. Many clubs will also finance and run schemes for young and disadvantaged people in their local communities.

A groundsman uses a blower to dry the markings on a pitch before a match at the Luzhniki Stadium in Moscow, Russia. Hundreds of people are employed to make sure that each game of football passes safely and efficiently.

Money-makers

Top football clubs earn their money from three areas. These are selling the television rights to show matches, revenue from ticket sales and income from commercial activities, such as merchandising and sponsorship.

Commercial revenue

Commercial staff at a club work hard to maximise the club's income. A stadium may be used to hold pop concerts, while luxurious seating at the ground is sold to companies wishing to entertain guests at a live match.

Football clubs also try to persuade companies to spend large sums of money buying blocks of seats at their grounds and to advertise inside the stadiums and on the players' shirts.

Alejandro Moreno of MLS side Columbus Crew. The team is sponsored by do-it-yourself store Glidden, which pays money to have its name on the club's shirts.

Matchday and merchandise

The money that fans pay to enter the stadium and watch the game can be a major part of the income a football club receives. Fans also tend to spend a lot of money inside the ground, buying match programmes, eating and drinking and visiting the club shop where they can buy merchandise. In grounds holding 60,000 spectators or more, it can add up. In the 2009–10 season, Manchester United raised £100.2 million in match day revenues alone. Sales of hats, books, replica kits and other merchandise are also very important. Teams bring out three or more complete kits every season and can sell tens of thousands of these items. Some kit manufacturers pay large sums to a club just for the right to make the kit.

Money box
Top five shirt sponsors in Europe (2010–11)

CLUB	SPONSOR	COST FOR THE SEASON
Barcelona	Qatar Foundation	£25 million
Bayern Munich	Deutsche Telekom	£23.6 million
Manchester United	Aon	£20 million
Liverpool	Standard Chartered Bank	£20 million
Real Madrid	BWIN	£16.8 million

Source: *Daily Telegraph*

Football and the media

The football media includes television, radio, websites, magazines and newspapers. They bring news to readers, viewers and listeners and put millions of pounds into the sport.

Broadcasting rights

Television, radio, mobile phone and Internet companies spend fortunes to gain the rights to broadcast football matches. At the start of the 2008–09 season, French football signed a deal worth £450 million every year with Canal Plus and Orange for the rights to show games. A similar deal for matches in the English Premier League is worth approximately double that. These sums are enormous, and on other continents, the figures are much smaller. The richest club in Morocco, Raja Casablanca, for example, earned a total of just £2.87 million from broadcasting, ticket and commercial sales in 2007.

Money box
Juventus is one of the most famous clubs in Italy, yet for some home matches it gets only a little more than 20,000 fans watching a match live at its ground. Over 60 per cent of the club's income each year comes from broadcasting rights.

Broadcasters around the world pay millions of pounds to show the biggest matches, such as the final of the UEFA Champions League, which saw English clubs Manchester United and Chelsea play each other in 2008.

Commentary and comment

The sports media commentate on live matches and review old games, as well as preview upcoming matches. Football is a sport which thrives on opinion. Which player is best? Which team will succeed? Opinions, match reports and interviews with players and coaches fill many pages of newspapers and occupy hours of radio and television programmes. Newspapers, television and radio all provide work for retired players and some current players. Top footballers' words and actions are followed in the media and reported across the world. Many players find the attention hard to deal with, but it is part of being a global football star.

> **"** *Sometimes, I'd like to have a conversation with a friend in a restaurant without feeling I'm being watched. At this rate I will have to go on holiday to Greenland. But maybe the Eskimos would know me.* **"**
>
> Spanish striker, **Fernando Torres**, on the pressures of fame and the media

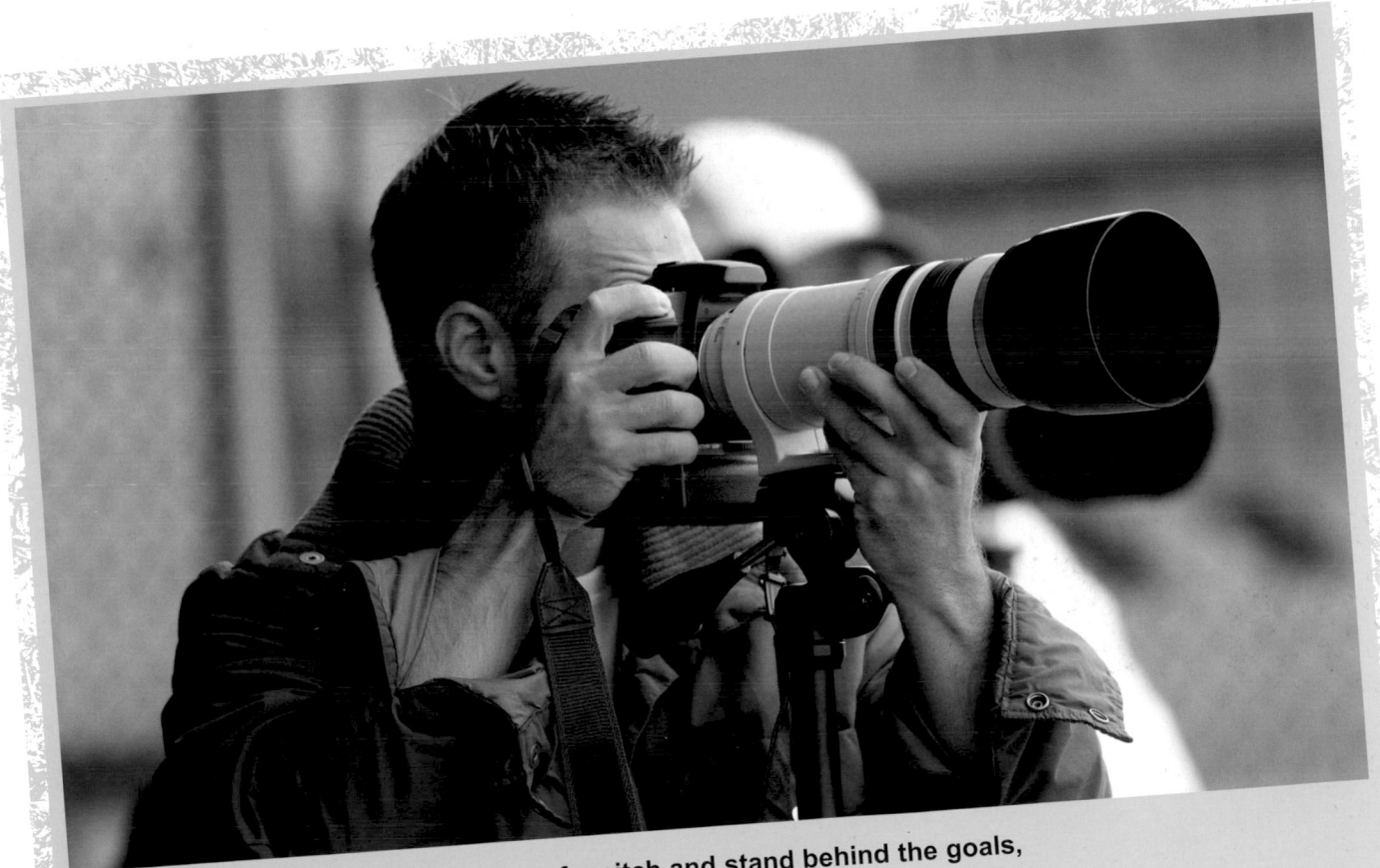

Sports photographers line the edge of a pitch and stand behind the goals, hoping to catch an important action shot from a match that they can sell to a photo agency, sports website, newspaper or magazine.

Players and agents

Today's footballers can earn millions of pounds every year from wages, sponsorships and advertising. Nearly all of the top players have agents who negotiate contracts and deals with clubs and sponsors on the players' behalf.

Rich rewards

Back in 1909, English player George Parsonage was banned from playing football for life. His crime was to ask for a £50 signing fee when he joined a new football club. Today, top players are multi-millionaires with contracts paying them more than £100,000 per week. The very best can double their salaries through contracts with sportswear manufacturers and other companies who pay the players to advertise their products. While women's football lags behind the men's game financially, the best female players can still earn substantial sums from companies sponsoring them. Marta Vieria da Silva from Brazil is one of the highest earners in women's football. Including her sponsorship deal with sports clothing company, Puma, she is believed to earn more than £25,000 per month.

A huge advertising billboard showing German goalkeeper Oliver Kahn. Sportswear manufacturer Adidas paid Kahn to use this image in the run-up to the 2006 World Cup in Germany.

> *Alongside my agent, Sir Alex Ferguson has been the most important person I've ever known in my career.*
>
> Manchester United's
> **Cristiano Ronaldo**

In 2008, Brazilian attacker Robinho signed for English club Manchester City. His agent was able to negotiate a weekly salary of £98,000.

Football agents

A player's agent is usually paid a percentage of the player's earnings, so the bigger the deal for the player, the more the agent will earn. As a result, agents are always pushing for better deals for players and have become a powerful force in the modern game. Some people have been critical of the agents' role, believing that agents' demands have helped to drive wages up and unsettle players into leaving one club for another.

Money box
Top 10 biggest earners in 2009

1.	**Lionel Messi** (Barcelona, Spain)	£29.7 million
2.	**David Beckham** (LA Galaxy, USA)	£27.3 million
3.	**Cristiano Ronaldo** (Real Madrid, Spain)	£27.0 million
4.	**Kaka** (Real Madrid, Spain)	£16.9 million
5.	**Thierry Henry** (Barcelona, Spain)	£16.2 million
6.	**Ronaldinho** (AC Milan, Italy)	£15.5 million
7.	**Carlos Tevez** (Manchester City, England)	£13.8 million
8.	**Zlatan Ibrahimovic** (Barcelona, Spain)	£13.0 million
9.	**Frank Lampard** (Chelsea, England)	£12.8 million
10.	**Samuel Eto'o** (Inter Milan, Italy)	£12.4 million

Source: *France Football Magazine*, 2010

Transfers

Football clubs change their squads of players by buying and selling footballers. These transactions are called transfers.

Reasons for moving

Footballers are transferred for many reasons including money, their performances and their relations with the coach. Clubs may sell a player they would like to keep if a large enough offer is made by another team. A club chairman or board of directors decides whether to sell or keep a player, but when a player wants to leave, this can cause problems. Players may wish to move to another club for a higher salary, to move back to their home country or to increase their chances of winning major competitions.

ON THE BALL

In 2004, Maribel Dominguez was bought by Mexican club, Celaya. She was the first woman to be transferred to a men's professional team. However, FIFA blocked the move.

Nicolas Anelka of France proved to be a bargain for English club Arsenal. In 1997, he was bought for £500,000 and then sold three years later to Real Madrid of Spain for £23 million.

Rising prices and value for money

The first known English transfer was Alf Common's move between Sheffield United and Sunderland for £520 in 1902. From the 1950s, prices for the leading players began to rise. The first million pound transfer was Giuseppe Savoldi's 1975 move between Italian clubs Bologna and Napoli, while Jean-Pierre Papin became the first £10 million player when he moved from Marseilles of France to AC Milan of Italy in 1992. Today, the richest clubs regularly spend £20 million on players, and build teams worth hundreds of millions of pounds.

Zinedine Zidane in action for the French national team. The gifted attacking midfielder was the world's most expensive player between 2001 and 2009, after his move from Juventus of Italy to Spanish club Real Madrid in 2001.

Money box
Top five most expensive transfers

PLAYER	FROM	TO	FEE
Christiano Ronaldo	Man United (England)	Real Madrid (Spain)	£80 million
Zlatan Ibrhimovic	Inter Milan (Italy)	Barcelona (Spain)	£56.5 million
Kaka	AC Milan (Italy)	Real Madrid (Spain)	£56 million
Fernando Torres	Liverpool (England)	Chelsea (England)	£50 million
Zinedine Zidane	Juventus (Italy)	Real Madrid (Spain)	£45.62 million

Source: *World Soccer* and *The Times*

The demand for players

The demand for new and better players to boost a football club's results is enormous. Some countries allow player transfers to occur only in short periods of the year, known as transfer windows.

Loan signings

Many clubs cannot afford to buy expensive players. Instead, they rely on borrowing players from other clubs. The club loaning the player out hopes that that player will build experience by playing regularly.

Loans can often last for just a few games or weeks, or even for a whole season. Often a clause is put in the loan contract, stopping the player from playing against their original club should the two teams meet. Some loan players later transfer permanently to their new clubs.

ON THE BALL

According to the Brazil Football Confederation, 1,017 footballers left Brazil in 2010 to play for teams abroad, many of them in Europe.

Argentinian player Javier Mascherano joined Liverpool on loan from West Ham in February 2007. Liverpool then bought him during the 2008–09 season. In 2010, he moved to Real Madrid.

Clubs go to great lengths to sign or develop young talent. Freddy Adu started his career at Major League Soccer team DC United in 2004. At the time, he was one of the world's youngest professional players, making his debut at the age of just 14.

I don't think that Europe will produce too many [new] players. The big ones will come from Africa and South America, which is why I do so much work in Brazil and Argentina.

Leading football agent,
Pini Zahavi

Player contracts and movement

Players will usually sign a contract, linking them to a club for a period of time. At the end of that time, they are free to move to another club. Many clubs choose to sell players who are nearing the end of contracts cheaply rather than let them go for free at the end. On the other hand, many players will wait until the end of their contracts and then move to other clubs for free. Because the new clubs have not had to pay millions of pounds to the old clubs, they can afford to pay the players a much higher salary. European clubs usually pay the highest wages, attracting players from all over the world. For example, 57 per cent of the 368 players at the 2010 African Cup of Nations played their club football in Europe.

Going global

Football is played in almost every country on the planet. Yet, many people are trying to promote football in places where business and football have rarely mixed, particularly in Africa, Asia and Oceania.

Expanding influence

The rise of television has brought the major leagues of Europe into homes all around the planet. As a result, major European clubs such as Real Madrid and Manchester United and players such as Cristiano Ronaldo and David Beckham have become famous brands. The clubs have tried to exploit this interest with tours and matches around the world. Organisations like FIFA have also promoted the sport worldwide with lots of different schemes and by holding competitions in Africa, Asia and North and South America.

ON THE BALL

The A-League in Australia has a salary system where each club has a set amount to spend on 19 of its players' wages. The wages of the club's 20th player can be unlimited.

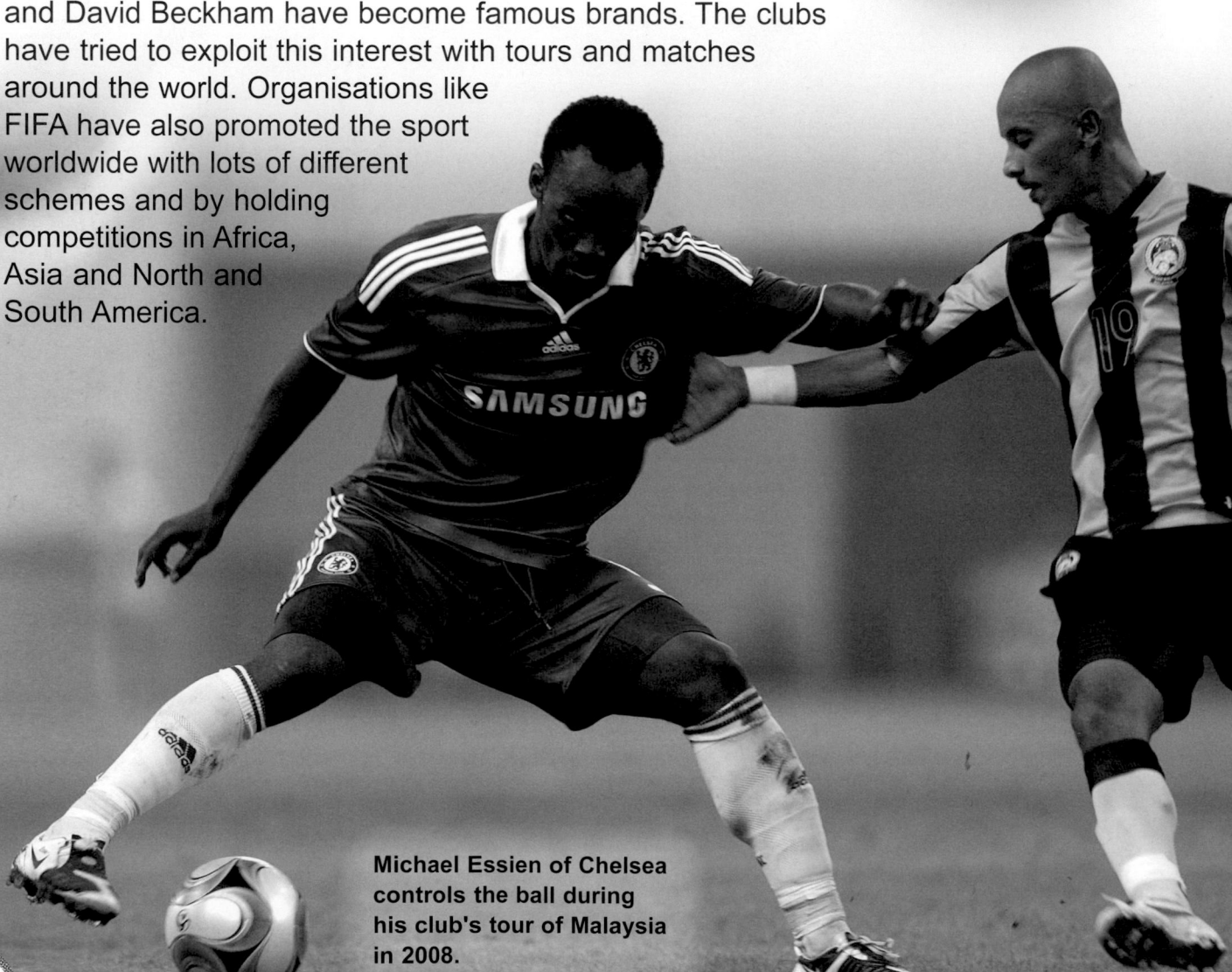

Michael Essien of Chelsea controls the ball during his club's tour of Malaysia in 2008.

David Beckham playing for MLS club LA Galaxy. Beckham is arguably the world's most famous footballer and, away from the pitch, is used to advertise a wide range of products in dozens of countries around the globe.

> *Asia holds huge potential for clubs hoping to expand their brand and business. There is incredible interest in the sport, the teams and the players. Our hope is that when someone in places like Korea, Japan or China thinks about American soccer, they think about the Galaxy.*
>
> Former President and General Manager of LA Galaxy,
> **Alexei Lalas**

New leagues and partnerships

In the past 15 years, several countries have tried to improve their elite or top football teams and players by starting a professional league. In Japan, the J-League has boomed in popularity since it began in 1993, as has MLS in the United States, whose games began three years later. The world's newest professional men's league, the A-League in Australia, began in 2005. Many major European teams have also formed partnerships with foreign clubs. For example, Dutch club Ajax partly owns South African club Ajax Cape Town.

Changing fortunes

Football is hugely competitive and this sees some teams rise and others fall over the seasons. With so much money involved, the pressures are enormous.

Rise and fall

Some teams have experienced a huge rise in their fortunes. La Paz FC was only formed in 1989, but has become one of the best sides in the Bolivian league. In contrast, some teams can fall away even more quickly. In 2001, English club Leeds United were in the Champions League semi final. Yet, within a few years, severe financial problems forced them to sell some of their best players and they were relegated twice.

ON THE BALL

Some leagues deduct points from a club when it goes into administration. Financially troubled English club Luton Town started the 2008-09 season on minus 30 points.

Italian team Napoli (in blue) has fallen and risen again in recent years. Originally a top team, the club went bankrupt in 2004. It reformed and has now risen back to the top Italian league, Serie A.

Poor performances bring pressure on players and coaches. Italian coach Roberto Donadoni (left) was dismissed after Italy's poor showing at Euro 2008, even though the team had won the World Cup two years earlier.

> **Unfortunately on our continent we have other priorities like health, education and development which are consuming our budget.**
>
> Angola national football team coach, **Luis Oliveira Goncalves**

In trouble

Struggling clubs are under great pressure to succeed. On very rare occasions, this can lead to clubs cheating by trying to fix the results of matches. Bernard Tapie, the former chairman of French club Marseille, was sent to jail in 1997 for bribing referees. In 2006, a major investigation into match-fixing at Italian Serie A clubs saw AC Milan docked points and kicked out of the Champions League, while Italian champions Juventus were docked points, stripped of their league title and immediately relegated to a lower division.

What it takes to be...

A club boss

Alexei Lalas

Lalas was a strong central defender who played for the United States team at the 1992 and 1996 Olympics and the 1994 World Cup. During his career, Lalas gained experience of world football playing in Ecuador and Italy, before becoming a fans' favourite at a number of MLS clubs. A spell as an analyst on television followed before appointments as general manager of three MLS clubs where he was responsible for the day-to-day running of the clubs' operations.

Career path

⚽ 1994: First American player in recent times to play for an Italian Serie A club.

⚽ 2004: Appointed General Manager of the MLS club, San Jose Earthquakes.

⚽ 2005: Became President and General Manager of New Jersey Metrostars.

⚽ 2006: Resigned to become General Manager of the Los Angeles Galaxy.

⚽ 2008: Left Los Angeles Galaxy and returned to work as a football analyst.

Alexei Lalas played an important role in David Beckham's move from Spanish club Real Madrid to the Los Angeles Galaxy in 2007.

Glossary

agent someone who negotiates on a player's behalf, ensuring that they get the best deal from clubs and sponsors.

amateur someone who plays a sport for enjoyment and is not paid for doing so.

coach someone who just works with the players, deciding who should play and what tactics to use, but who does not get involved in any business aspects of the football club.

league a group of teams that play each other to decide their standing in a league table. The team that wins the most stands at the top of this table, while the team that loses the most sits at the bottom and may be relegated to a lower league.

manager someone who oversees the running of a football team, deciding which players play and which tactics to use, and also gets involved in some of the business decisions, such as which players to buy and sell.

merchandise clothing, toys, flags and anything else that a football club can put its name, colours or badge on and sell to fans to raise money.

professional someone who is paid for playing a sport.

season the continuous run of games over an entire year.

season ticket a ticket that allows a fan to watch all of the games at a team's home stadium throughout an entire season.

sponsorship When a company pays to use a club's logo or a player's name or face to promote its products.

Books

Sporting Skills: Football by Clive Gifford (Wayland, 2008)
Talking about Football: Manager by Antony Lishak (Franklin Watts, 2006)
Training to Succeed: Football by Edward Way (Franklin Watts, 2009)
Inside Sport: Football by Clive Gifford (Wayland, 2007)

Websites

www.footballeconomy.com
All about football finance and business.
www.fourfourtwo.com
Packed full of transfer news and views.

www.thefa.com
Information on how to get involved in football, including finding your local club and the qualifications needed to coach.

Index